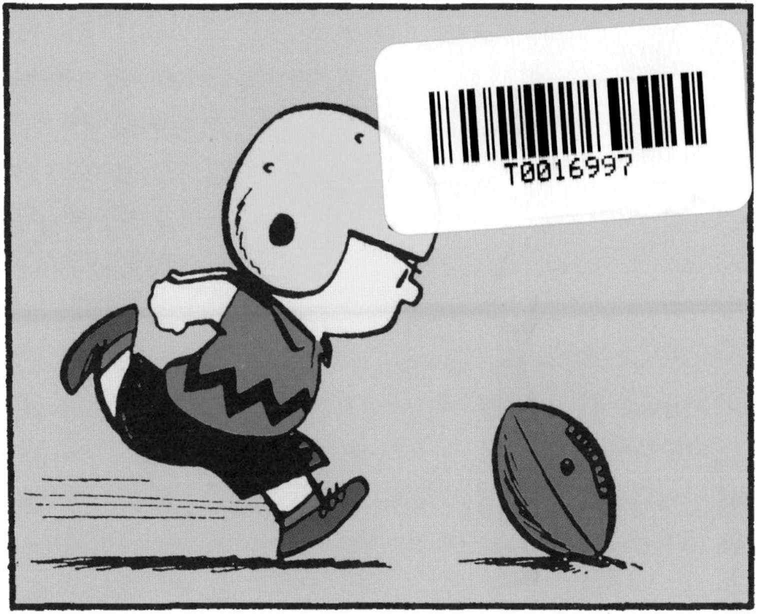

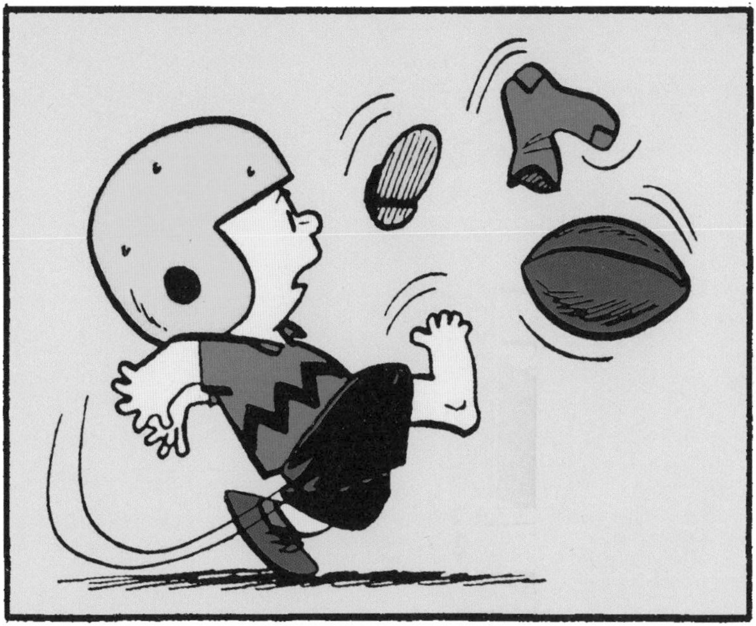

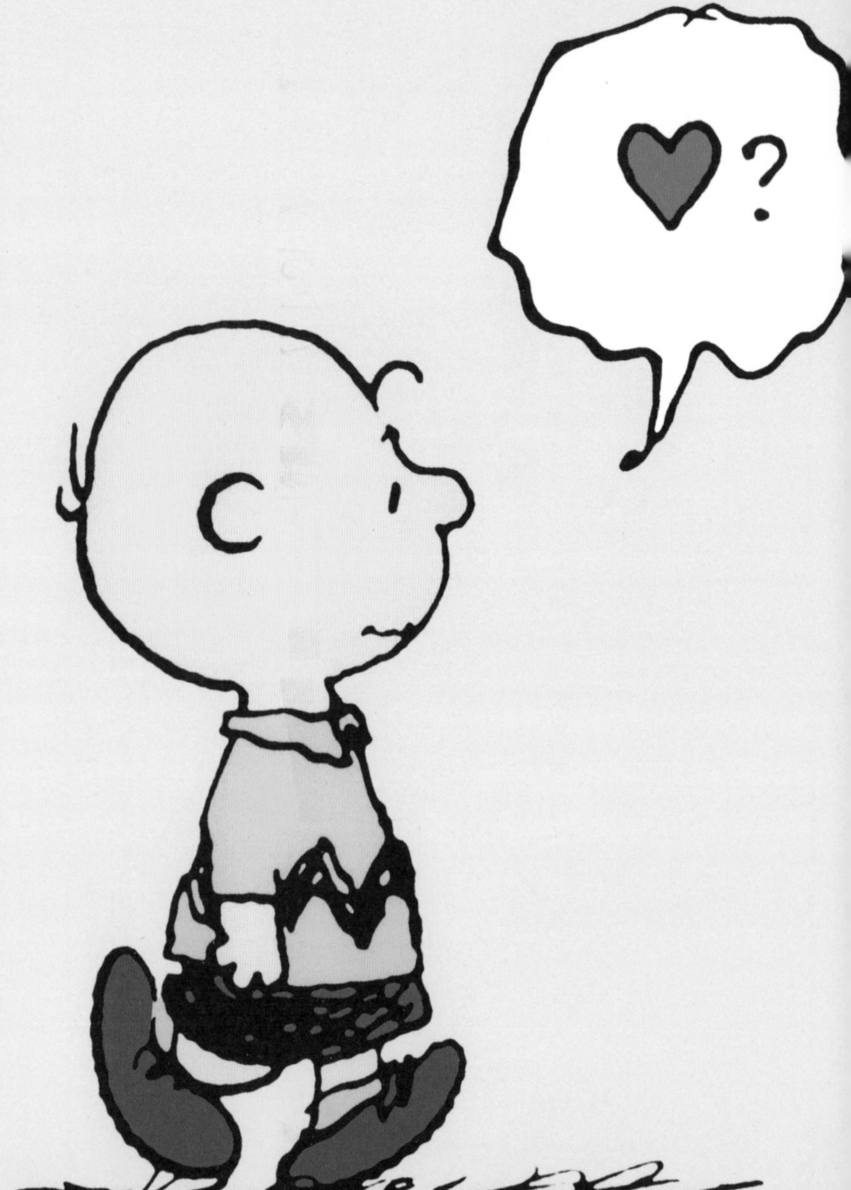

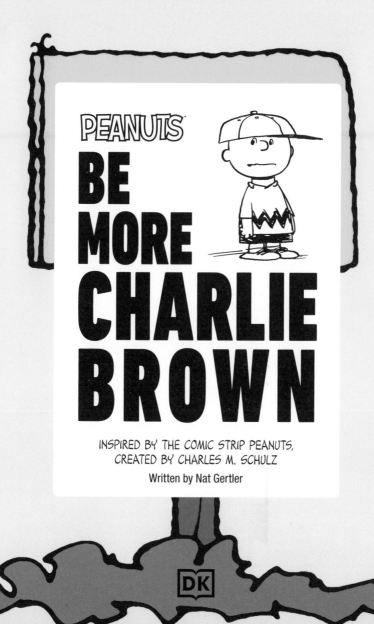

PEANUTS™

BE MORE CHARLIE BROWN

INSPIRED BY THE COMIC STRIP PEANUTS,
CREATED BY CHARLES M. SCHULZ

Written by Nat Gertler

DK

CONTENTS

DIG DEEP AND BOUNCE BACK

We are all somewhat Charlie Brown. When Charlie Brown has the football pulled away or sees his romantic crush ignore him, it reminds us of our own struggles. We all get our metaphorical kite stuck in the metaphorical tree at times. Being a human is, to some degree, being Charlie Brown. The question is, what do you do about it?

You could try to step away from it, to deny the "Charlie Brownness" in your soul. But maybe that isn't so wise, because Charlie Brown's strategies seem to work. He always gets past a failure, even if another awaits him down the road. Faced with being somewhat Charlie Brown, the wisest path might be to *Be More Charlie Brown*.

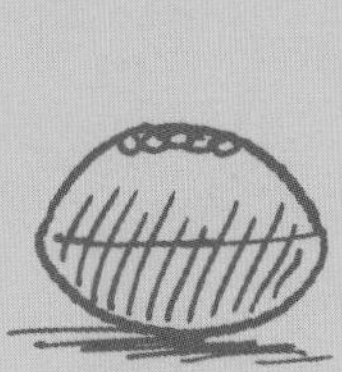

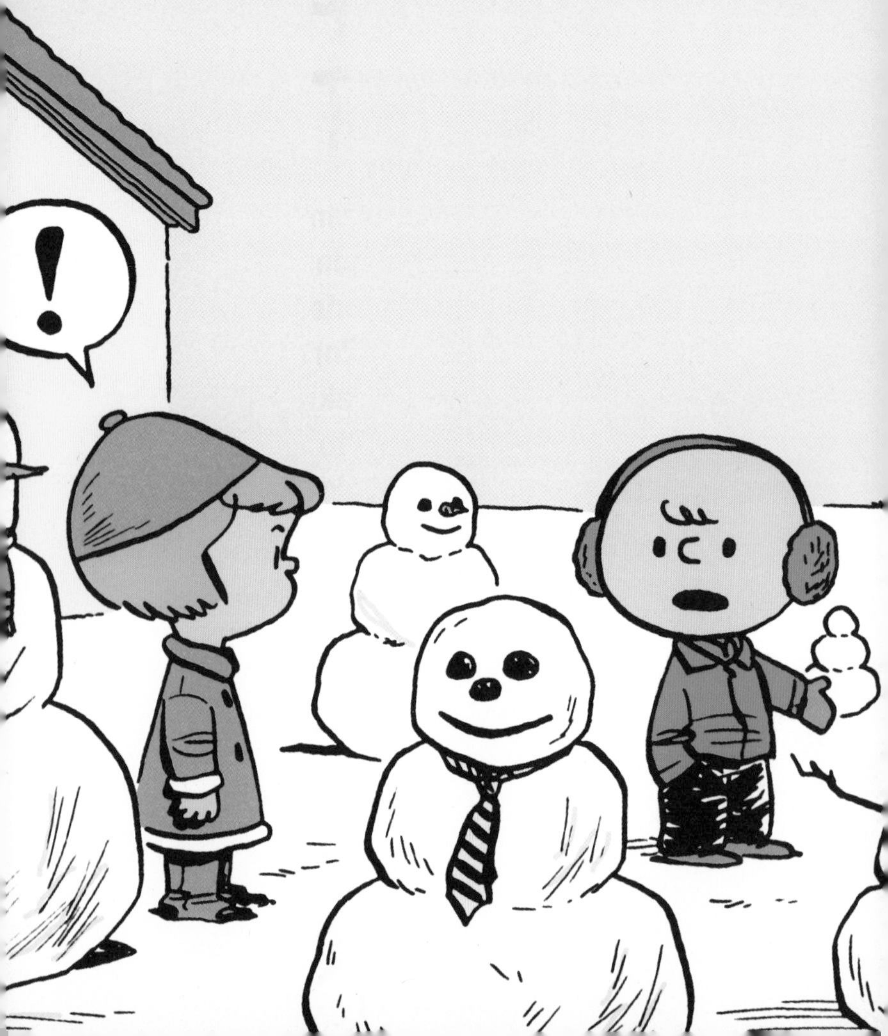
!

MAKE THE EFFORT

Trying hard does not guarantee you will succeed, but not trying guarantees you won't. Don't let the magnitude of a task intimidate you. When the effort required seems overwhelming, try taking it one piece at a time. The journey to a hundred snowmen starts with a single snowball.

"I'M AFRAID IF I GIVE THIS BOX OF CANDY TO THAT LITTLE RED-HAIRED GIRL, SHE'LL JUST LAUGH IN MY FACE."

Charlie Brown

LOVE IS HARD.
LOVE HARD ANYWAY.

Love is risky. You put your heart out there,
knowing that your own equivalent to Charlie Brown's
Little Red-Haired Girl might leave it battered, bruised,
or even broken. It can be tempting to play it safe,
to not love. But the heart is a muscle, and like all
muscles, it needs exercise. Take a chance at love.
You might win, and if you don't, you learn. You learn
that those you love are not perfect, like Charlie Brown
learns his Little Red-Haired Girl nibbles on her pencils.
And if you are capable of loving a flawed human,
then your flawed self is capable of being loved.

"I WAS GETTING SO SICK OF THAT
SILLY BLACK STRIPE."
Violet

LET YOUR STYLE
BE YOUR STYLE

Charlie Brown's zig-zag shirts may not be fashionable. They may never have been fashionable and may never become fashionable—but that's okay.

"Fashion" is just what everyone else is wearing. What Charlie Brown has is *style*. He has a look all his own. You could find one of his shirts and know it was *his* shirt. He's not worried about being like everyone else or copying what others are doing. Why take on all that work and face those constantly changing expectations? No, Charlie Brown just keeps on being Charlie Brown, and that works for him.

Find your style and let it work for you.

"THE THREE MOST
BEAUTIFUL WORDS IN THE
ENGLISH LANGUAGE!"
Snoopy

FEED THE DOG

Life gives us all responsibilities. You may have
bills to pay, errands to run, or pet beagles to feed.
These responsibilities may be things you don't enjoy
doing, but you are going to have to do them anyway.
Whether or not you enjoy feeding the dog does not
matter. The dog must be fed. Charlie Brown knows
that putting off a tedious task won't make things
better—the responsibility will just hang over his
head, getting heavier and heavier until it's done.
So Charlie Brown gripes and scowls, but he gripes and
scowls while getting the job done. And the dog gets fed.

"I ACTUALLY BELIEVE THAT
I CAN FLY THIS KITE!"
Charlie Brown

DEDICATION IS SUCCESS

Charlie Brown's kite-flying skills are amazing.
He can land a kite right in the sewer, entangle all the
neighborhood kids in the string, and keep the local
Kite-Eating Tree well fed. Some see this inability
to do the usual "keep the kite in the air" thing as
a failure. That point of view is understandable, but
it's wrong. Charlie Brown is never truly defeated.
He's always ready to buy one more kite and make
one more attempt to place it in the sky. As long
as you keep your hope alive and keep striving
for your goal, you won't truly lose.

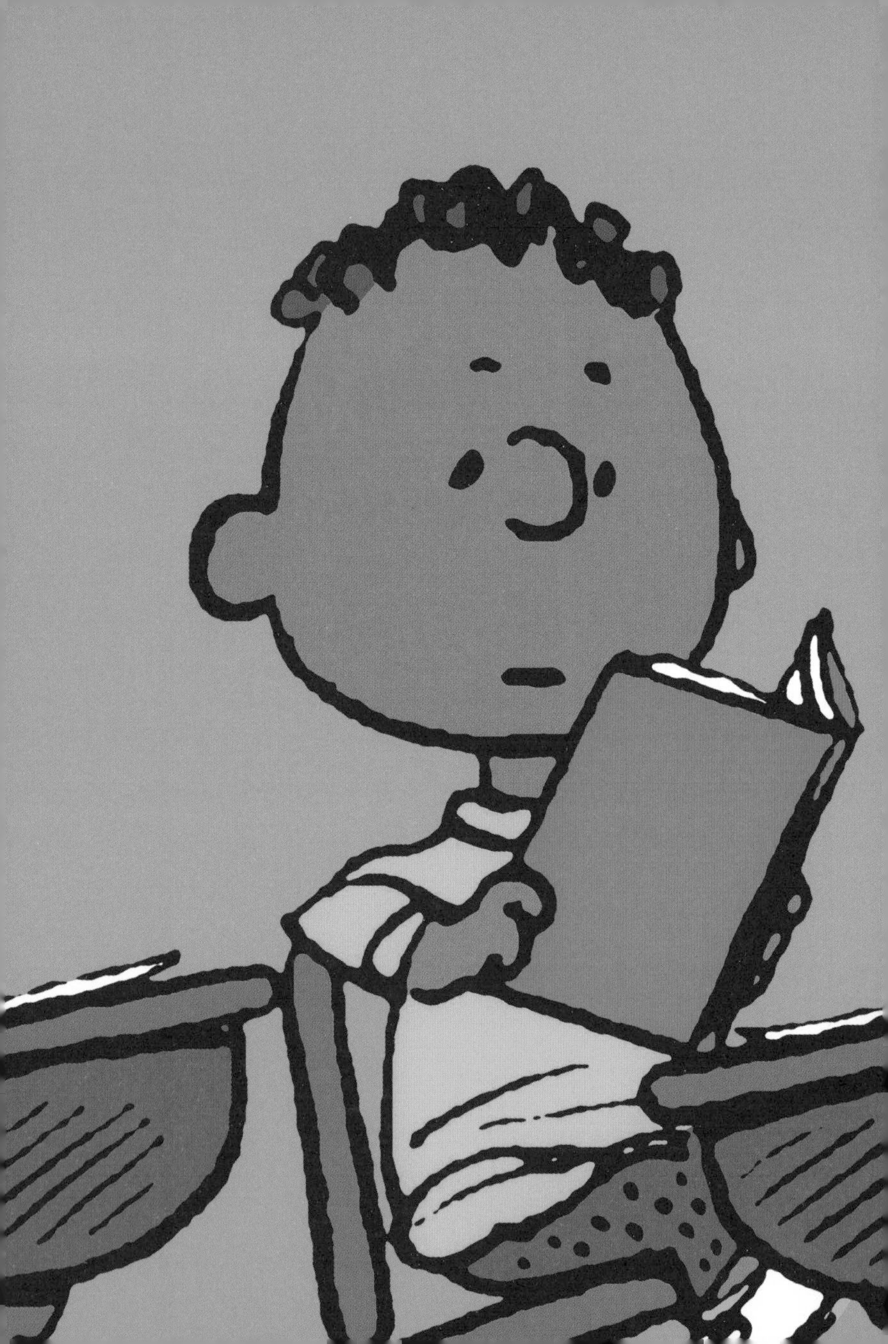

KEEP LEARNING

If you think you have nothing left to learn, then you've got something to learn. Getting an education may seem inconvenient or even painful sometimes, but it prepares you for life ahead. Whether you're in the classroom or out in whatever windy streets life leads you down, never stop learning.

"I'M MAKING MY OWN SET OF FLASHCARDS."

Linus

STUDY WISELY

Learning isn't just memorizing things. Questioning facts and requesting more information can be just as important. Charlie Brown recognizes the words on the flashcards Linus is showing him, but he can't accept the spellings. That word isn't really spelled "welkum," is it? Meanwhile, Linus feels that he cannot learn his lines for the Christmas pageant until he can understand exactly what it's about. Who was Jeremiah? Where was Rama? Why was Rachel so upset? Don't be content to just accept information. The more questions you ask, the more understanding you'll gain.

"I'M TEACHING LINUS SOME LITTLE-KNOWN FACTS OF SCIENCE."

Lucy

VALUE EXPERTISE

The world is filled with folks who are willing to tell you things. Deciding which of them to listen to can be a problem. You might want to steer clear of the self-appointed science expert who just makes things up, or the World Famous Attorney who looks a lot like Snoopy in a bowler hat. Even a smart kid like Linus may lead you astray about what happens in a sincere pumpkin patch on Halloween night. But once you find a true expert—perhaps someone like Peppermint Patty, who is not book-smart but knows how to strike you out in three straight pitches—pay attention. These are people you can learn from.

"ONCE I THOUGHT I HEARD A JET
FLYING OVER OUR SCHOOL. I TURNED
AROUND, AND IT WAS YOU SNORING..."
Franklin

PAY ATTENTION

School can be tough. As Peppermint Patty can tell
you, it's easy to be lulled to sleep and find yourself
waking up shouting a string of random answers,
hoping one of them matches some question you
didn't hear. But if you pay attention, you may learn
how wide the Mississippi River is, how fierce gully
cats are, or even just *how* to pay attention. By paying
attention, you can get the most from school and from
life, whether you're like Franklin who gains knowledge
for its own sake, or like Sally who attends school
only "to become rich and famous." If you don't pay
attention, you literally don't know what you're missing.

"I ADMIRE ALL TEACHERS,
BUT MISS OTHMAR IS
A GEM AMONG GEMS..."

Linus

RESPECT YOUR TEACHER

Teachers endure a lot. They have to deal with sleeping students like Peppermint Patty, screaming students like Sally, and students like Linus, who keeps on forgetting to bring the promised eggshells for the class diorama. Occasionally, they might even have to deal with fuzzy-faced beagles who have snuck into class. Yet despite all those distractions, they somehow still find the energy to give lessons, grade tests, and even host show-and-tell. Teachers are deserving of your admiration, your respect, and you finally remembering to bring in those eggshells.

"I LEARNED A LOT IN SCHOOL TODAY. I LEARNED ALL ABOUT TRANSPORTATION."

Sally

LEARN BY EXPERIENCE

Life is a sequence of experiences. Go through life with eyes wide open and you can learn valuable things. Good experiences teach you that something you did worked—that you got it right. Pigpen learns that it's okay if he shows up as his usual filthy self to a birthday party, so long as the present is clean. That's a good experience. But even bad experiences can be valuable in the long run. They teach you what you should never do again. Missing the bus and having to get to school by foot will give you one bad day, but it's a bad day you likely won't repeat. The worst experiences can be the best lessons.

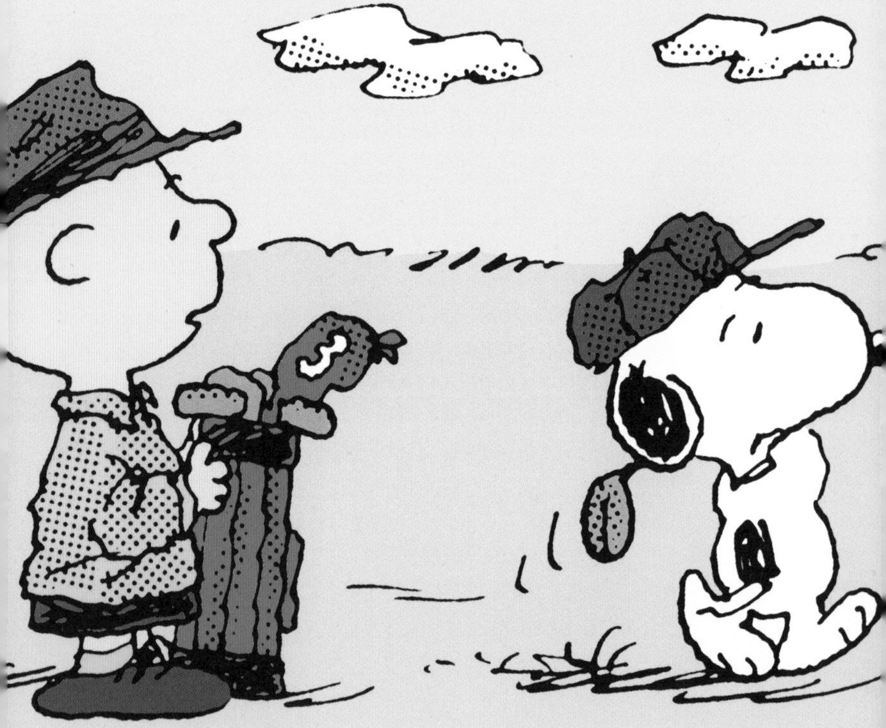

FOLLOW A PHILOSOPHY

A philosophy gives you a perspective through which to view the world. You may have one grand philosophy that covers everything, such as Charlie Brown's view that "life is like a golf course." Or maybe you have a series of smaller philosophies, like viewing golf as only a game and knowing that it's worth talking to your dog even if he can't respond. Find the truths that work for you.

"I'VE DEVELOPED A
NEW PHILOSOPHY..."
Charlie Brown

HAVE A PHILOSOPHY

Everyone should have a philosophy. Whether it's
a carefully charted view of the world or a mere motto,
it helps in making decisions. They can be decisions
of action, like when Snoopy thinks "Should I steal
Linus's security blanket?" Or they can be decisions
of reaction, like when Linus thinks "Snoopy has my
blanket! How should I feel about that?" Philosophies
are very personal. Charlie Brown's decision to dread
solely in the moment sounds downbeat, but it frees
him from having to dread all the things coming next
week. Find a philosophy that serves your life as well
as Charlie Brown's dread-based view serves his.

"WHY ARE YOU
TELLING ME?"
Charlie Brown

SHARE YOUR PHILOSOPHY

Be like Sally: eager to share your philosophy.
Letting someone in on your philosophy might help
them enhance theirs—or at least just understand
you a little better. Putting your philosophy into words
will also force you to examine it clearly and perhaps
to recognize its weaknesses. If you don't see any
weaknesses yourself, a friend might do that for you.
Charlie Brown's lack of interest in hearing Sally's
philosophy "Details at eleven!" might be just the
thing to let his sister know it's a philosophy
best abandoned at 10:45.

"THERE'S A DIFFERENCE BETWEEN A PHILOSOPHY AND A BUMPER STICKER!"

Linus

ENDURE NAYSAYERS

Not everyone will understand your philosophy.
The fussbudgets and well-meaning friends in your
life may even tell you that your philosophy is wrong.
Sometimes quite loudly. Don't let them get you down.
Remember, it's your philosophy, not theirs, so it only
has to make sense to you. Let them find their own
philosophy. And if they call you "blockhead" for
finding what works for you? Well, just block it out—
and remember that it doesn't change the fact that
you, like Charlie Brown, might actually have
the roundest head in town.

"IT'S A PHILOSOPHY, SIR. IT SAYS THAT
IF YOU DENY SOMETHING EXISTS,
THEN IT DOESN'T EXIST."

Marcie

LIVE YOUR WORDS

Let your philosophy enter not just your mind, but your whole life. Philosophies need to be applied to be effective. If you believe that happiness is a warm puppy, then go and find that warm puppy and let him make you happy. What if your philosophy lets you down? When Linus put "let a smile be your umbrella" to the test, he found that a smile actually makes a lousy umbrella. The only thing to do is learn from it, adjust your philosophy to your new understanding of the world—maybe a slightly less literal one—and move on. But if mere disbelief might make those D-minuses disappear as Marcie believes, it's worth a try!

"THE BEST WAY TO SOLVE
PROBLEMS IS TO AVOID THEM."
Linus

ALLOW YOURSELF ESCAPE

You cannot cure all the problems in the world—not
even all those in your own little slice of it. If you fight
every difficulty head-on, you face an endless war.
Deal with the problems you have to, solve the ones
you can ... but also give yourself the freedom to duck
a problem and let it fly right by you. Walk away from
those arguments that don't really need to be won.
Ignore that cat next door. Put off until tomorrow what
you aren't equipped to deal with today. Like Linus,
run away from the problems that you can outpace.
The exercise will do you good.

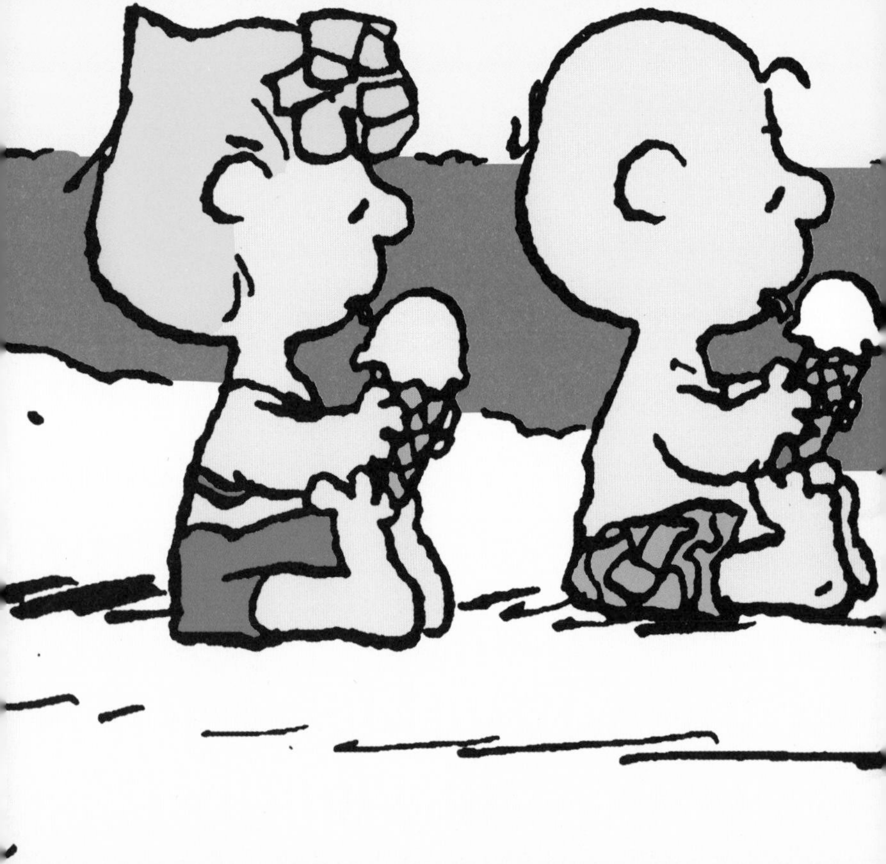

TAKE CARE OF YOURSELF

Life is filled with things and people you have to take care of. Never forget that *you* are on that list of people. Your needs and desires are just as important as anyone else's, so give yourself a break and attend to them. If you don't take care of yourself and treat yourself well, you soon won't be in shape to help others.

"YOU KNOW, I FEEL
BETTER ALREADY!"
Charlie Brown

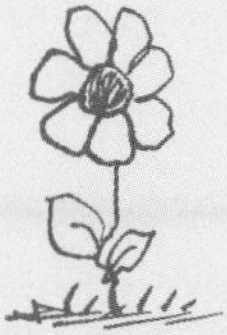

SPEND THE NICKEL

Sometimes you may face stresses and emotions that are more than you can handle. Professional therapists are available to help. You just need to find the right one for you. Lucy is not the best therapist in the world (although she does offer affordable pricing and a convenient location). Even so, not only Charlie Brown but also Linus, Sally, Pigpen, Schroeder, Frieda, and even Snoopy have used her services. A listening ear can be as valuable as advice given. Therapy can get you through tough times and show you ways to deal with stress. There is no shame in reaching out for help. So reach out.

"I'M GOING TO HAVE TO LIE HERE
FOR THE REST OF MY LIFE."
Charlie Brown

GET UP AGAIN

Life will knock you down. You know the feeling.
That feeling when the football of life is pulled out
from in front of you and you are sent flying through
the air, just waiting for cruel, cruel gravity to bring
you slamming back to the ground. Flat on your back
again, staring up at the skies, you may wonder if this
time you should just stay there. But consider this:
if life has knocked you down a hundred times,
that means you, like Charlie Brown, have already
gotten back up ninety-nine. You have it in you.
Keep that streak going.

"ONLY ONE YARD OF OUTING FLANNEL
STANDS BETWEEN ME AND A
NERVOUS BREAKDOWN!"

Linus

FIND YOUR SECURITY BLANKET

Maybe you are like Linus and you find comfort in a physical object like a light blue blanket that feels so soft against your cheek. Perhaps there are sounds that bring comfort to your inner Schroeder, such as a lulling symphony by a favorite composer. You may even have places you go to for peace, like Snoopy's cozy spot at the peak of his doghouse. The world is tough sometimes, so it's important to know what sets you at ease. On a nice day, take that solitary time in your favorite spot—it may make the day just a little bit nicer. And on a tough day, turn up your favorite Beethoven record—it may just carry you through.

"WELL HELLO THERE,
CHARLIE BROWN, YOU BLOCKHEAD!!"
Charlie Brown

UNDERSTAND HOW OTHERS SEE YOU

Everybody you meet has their own view of you.
It doesn't mean they are right, but it's still important
to understand how they see you. It helps you decide
how to interact with them. Once you realize they think
you're a blockhead, you can let it go or you can try
to disprove it. Just don't let those other people's
opinions define you. Peppermint Patty may think
Snoopy is a funny-looking kid with a big nose, but
he is still a dog. Charlie Brown may wish he had
a normal dog like everybody else, but Snoopy
keeps on being the imaginative beagle that he is.
Understand others, but don't lose sight of yourself.

"A GOOD WAY TO FORGET A LOVE
AFFAIR IS TO EAT A LOT OF GOOP!"
Charlie Brown

KNOW WHAT WORKS FOR YOU

The world is full of people offering advice. Why, you
may even be holding a self-help book in your hands
right now! But no strategy works for everybody.
Only you can tell if a piece of advice is good for you.
Charlie Brown knows that a good dose of discount
goop will clear away his broken heart. Linus knows
that drawing people standing with their hands behind
their backs hides the fact that he can't draw hands.
Schroeder knows to keep a closet full of backup
Beethoven statues in case a spurned would-be
girlfriend smashes one with a baseball bat. Their ways
won't work for you. Find your own strategies that will.

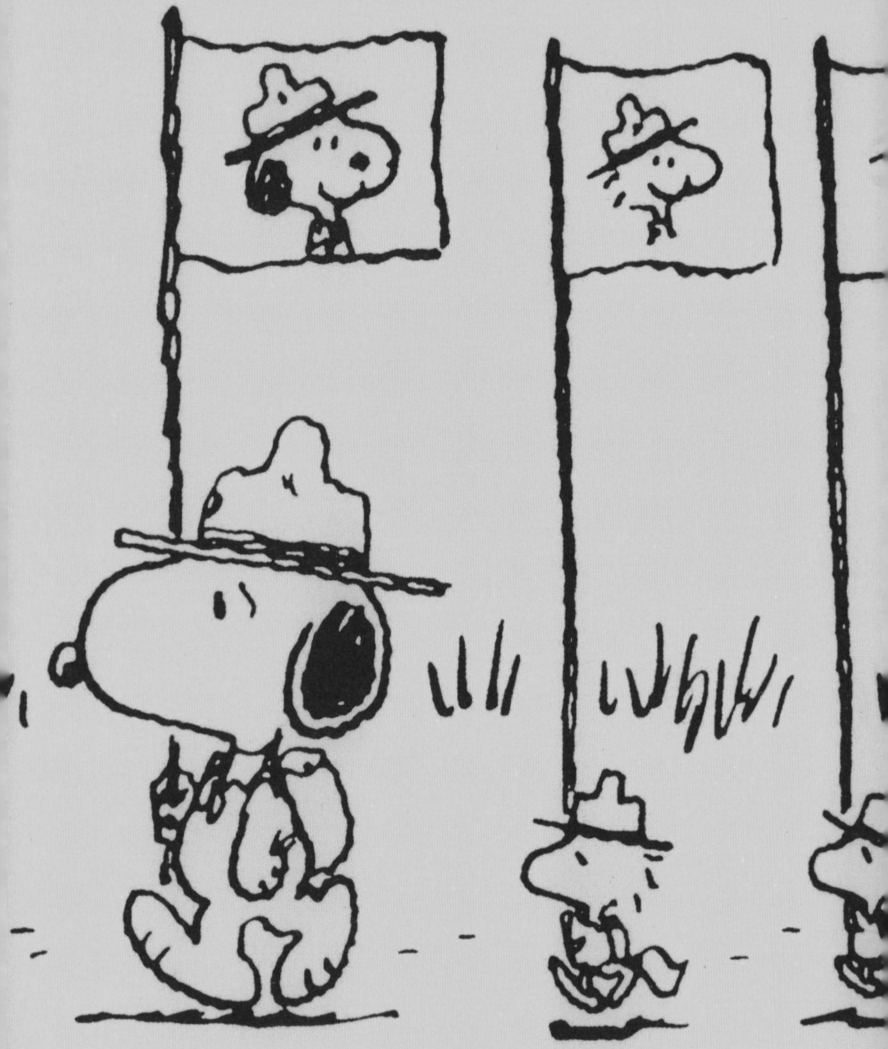

VALUE OTHERS

No man is an island, and no Beagle Scout is a troop of one. You deal with many people in your life. The more you can understand them and accept them, the richer your life will be. You might even find someone special (whether it be your friend of friends or your sweet babboo) along the way.

"I NEED ALL THE FRIENDS
I CAN GET."
Charlie Brown

SURROUND YOURSELF
WITH INTERESTING PEOPLE

There's nothing wrong with friends who are a lot like you—the fact that you have a lot in common will help you understand each other and share things with ease. But if you can make friends with one person who turns dirt into mud pies and another who turns it into a fashion statement; with a thumb-sucking theologian and an award-winning fussbudget; and with an up-and-coming concert pianist and a delusional dog, then you'll have a good variety of people in your life. Compatriots who introduce you to different experiences and alternative perspectives will always make your life richer.

"OTHER KIDS' BASEBALL HEROES
HIT HOME RUNS... MINE GETS
SENT DOWN TO THE MINORS!"
Charlie Brown

RESPECT EFFORT

Charlie Brown's hero isn't very good at winning.
While other ballplayers get picked for the All-Star
Game, Joe Shlabotnik gets kicked off the team and
sent down to the Green Grass league. And when he
works his way back up to the big league, he just gets
sent down again. But the thing is, he keeps trying.
This makes him a perfect hero for Charlie Brown, who
knows he's not a winner either but takes ol' Joe as
inspiration to keep trying. Anyone can value people
who have reached the top—who never seem to take
a false step. They are adored by millions. Why not
admire those who struggle but persist? Then you
will have worthwhile heroes indeed.

"PATRICIA IS AN UNUSUAL GIRL.
DID YOU KNOW SHE NEVER ONCE
CRITICIZED MY APPEARANCE?"

Pigpen

FIND THE GOOD IN ALL

It's easy to spot the worst aspect of a person: the layer of dirt, the loud mouth, a somber expression. Don't let that first impression keep you from seeing the better aspects that lurk inside. And once you find that good, let them know about it! Sure, some folks may already have pride in what they think is their best attribute—like Frieda loves her naturally curly hair, for example—but others might not be aware that they are truly kind, purely supportive, and genuinely the best of friends. Sharing your insight into what makes them special may help them through a moment when they are feeling the worst about themselves.

"OF COURSE, HE'S REALLY A PEN-PAL.
BUT I CALL HIM PENCIL-PAL BECAUSE
I CAN'T WRITE WITH A PEN."
Charlie Brown

REACH OUT

We all need to feel connected. Take the time to stay
in touch with your friends. Ask them how they are and
tell them what's going on in your life. Did you win the
spelling bee? Did you lose the election? Do you feel
like you can't talk to the Little Red-Haired Girl of your
dreams? Share your humanity, and give your friends
a chance to share theirs. If communication sometimes
seems hard, remember—there's always a way.
Snoopy only thinks his sentences and Woodstock only
speaks bird, but somehow they manage to have
whole conversations. Just reach out. The response
you get may gladden your heart.

"THIS TIME I'M REALLY GONNA
KICK THAT FOOTBALL!"
Charlie Brown

RISK BELIEVING IN PEOPLE

Time after time, Lucy pulls the ball away just as
Charlie Brown is about to kick it, sending him flying
through the air. And time after time, Charlie Brown
lets Lucy talk him into trying again. Sure, Charlie
Brown has noticed the pattern. But deep down inside
himself, he believes in humanity. He believes people
are capable of correcting themselves and making
better decisions. So he gives Lucy a second, a third,
and a thirty-seventh chance to hold the football
for him, because not doing that would mean giving
up on hope. Keep faith that people can improve.
If you believe that about others, you'll also
believe it about yourself.

"HERE YOU GO, RERUN. I WON
BACK ALL YOUR MARBLES."
Charlie Brown

BE THERE WHEN NEEDED

Charlie Brown may seem wishy-washy and sometimes uninvolved—but when someone can use his help, he's there. He was there when Peppermint Patty needed a mascot. He was there when a group of little kids wanted to learn baseball. He even took care of things when the local marble hustler bullied young Rerun Van Pelt out of his marbles. When faced with someone who needs a hand, it might be tempting to turn away and hope that others will help them out. That's an easy route to take. But it's better to be more Charlie Brown.

Penguin
Random
House

Senior Editor Ruth Amos
Designer Rosamund Bird
Senior Designer Clive Savage
Senior Production Editor Jennifer Murray
Senior Production Controller Mary Slater
Managing Editor Emma Grange
Managing Art Editor Vicky Short
Publishing Director Mark Searle

DK would like to thank Nat Gertler for his text, Craig Herman
at Peanuts Worldwide, Alexis Fajardo and Alena Carnes of
Charles M. Schulz Creative Associates, Julia March and Pamela Afram
for editorial assistance, and Kayla Dugger for proofreading.

First American Edition, 2022
Published in the United States by DK Publishing
1450 Broadway, Suite 801, New York, NY 10018

Page design copyright © 2022 Dorling Kindersley Limited
DK, a Division of Penguin Random House LLC
22 23 24 25 26 10 9 8 7 6 5 4 3 2 1
001–327479–Jun/2022

A catalog record for this book is available
from the Library of Congress.
ISBN: 978-0-7440-5463-7

DK books are available at special discounts when purchased in bulk
for sales promotions, premiums, fund-raising, or educational use.
For details, contact: DK Publishing Special Markets,
1450 Broadway, Suite 801, New York, NY 10018
SpecialSales@dk.com

Printed and bound in China

For the curious

www.dk.com
www.peanuts.com

MIX
Paper from
responsible sources
FSC™ C018179

This book is made from
Forest Stewardship Council™
certified paper—one small
step in DK's commitment
to a sustainable future.

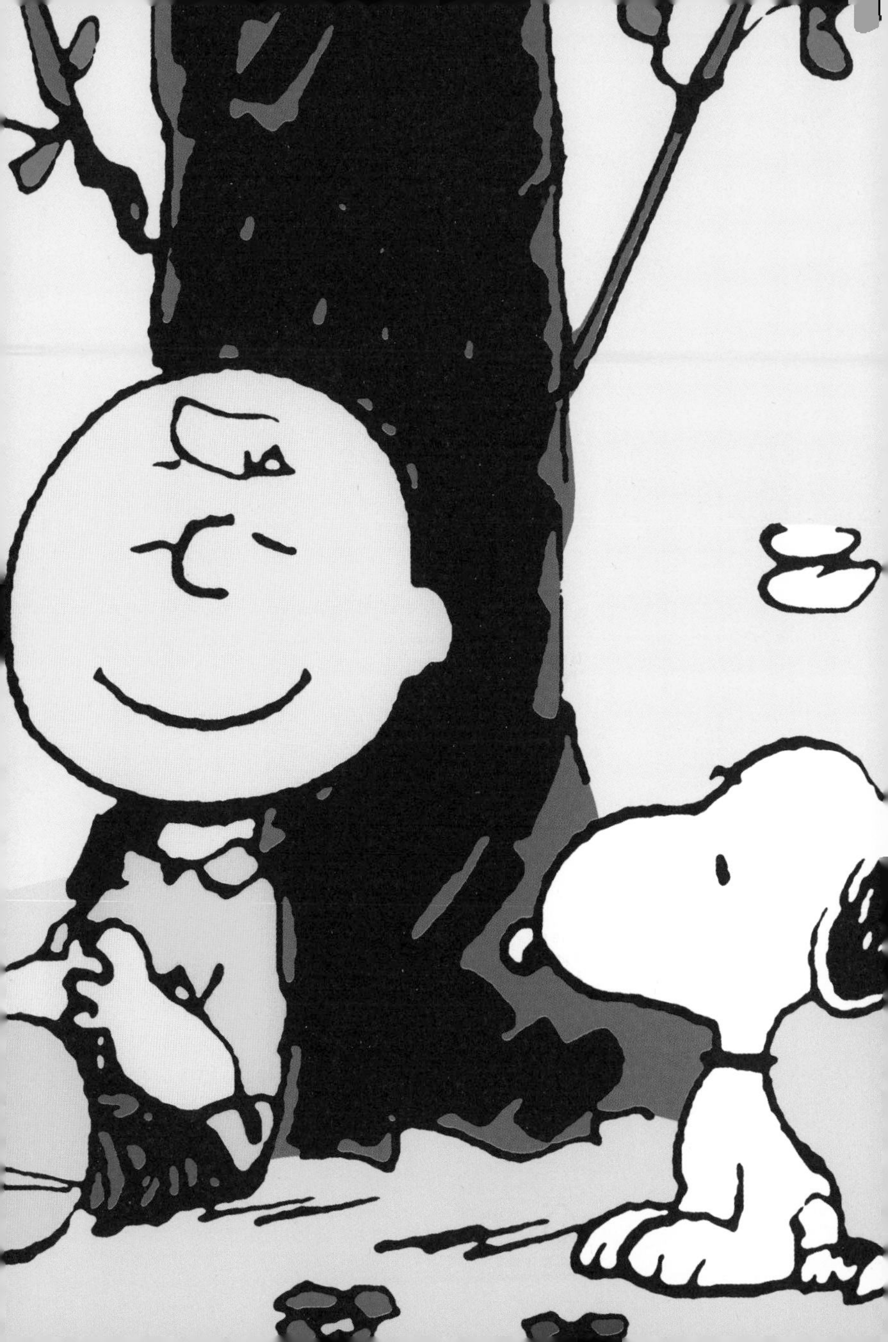

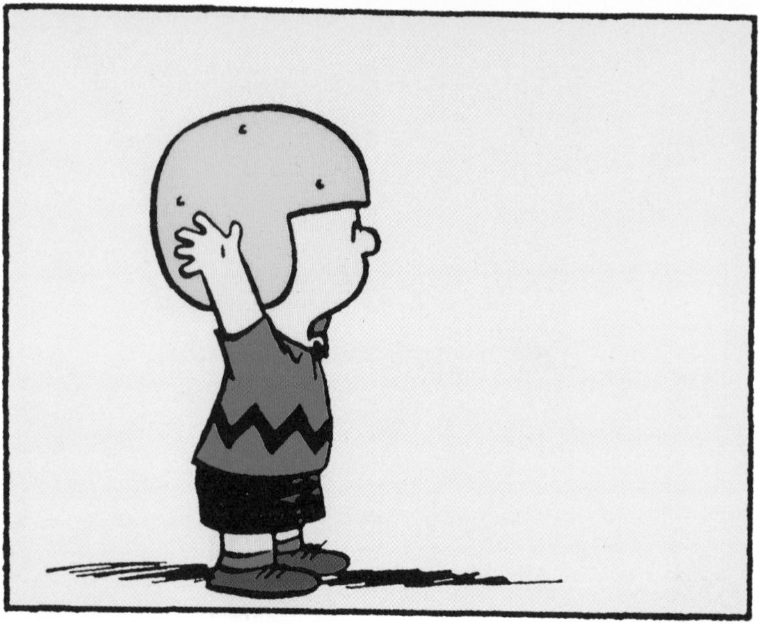

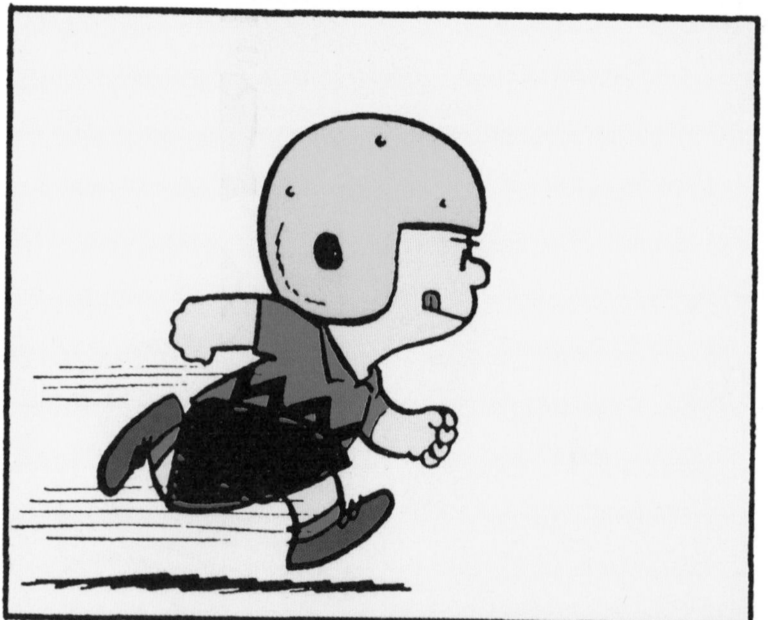